Moto G P
Complete User Manual
For Beginners and
Seniors

A Complete Step-by-Step User
Guide With Tips & Tricks to Use
Your Phone With Ease

Wesley K. Jackson

Table of Contents

Introduction

The User Guide for the Motorola G Power Series: A Comprehensive Guide to Getting the Most Out of Your Device

We would like to take this opportunity to welcome you to the Moto G Power User Guide, which is your ultimate companion for maximizing the capacity of your smartphone. This guide is intended to assist you in navigating every feature, option, and secret trick that your smartphone has to offer, regardless of whether you are looking to use your Moto G Power for the first time or are an experienced enthusiast.

With its strong performance, beautiful display, and adaptable camera system, the Moto G Power is a smartphone that offers all of these features at a price that is not prohibitive. In order to get the most out of your phone, however, you need to have a solid understanding of its capabilities. With this book, you will get detailed instructions, useful suggestions, and professional guidance on a variety of topics, including: Getting Started: Initialize your device, transfer data, and customize your home screen to suit your preferences.

The Moto G Power's multi-lens configuration is showcased in the book "Mastering the Camera," which provides expert advice on how to take great photographs and movies.

Discover the best practices for fast-charging and energy-saving ways to maximize the life of your cellular device's battery.

Security and privacy may be achieved by establishing fingerprint and face recognition, securing your data, and managing permissions for an application.

Hidden features and shortcuts are a means of unlocking secret tricks that can enhance your user experience and allow you to increase your productivity.

In order to ensure that your phone continues to function without any interruptions, it is essential to undertake troubleshooting and maintenance tasks.

This tutorial will guarantee that you become a Moto G Power in no time at all by providing you with easily understandable explanations, handy screenshots, and directions that are simple to follow.

Prepared to discover everything that your phone is capable of? It's time to get started!

Your adventure with the Moto G Power starts right now.

Chapter 1: Configure Your Phone

• **SIM and SD Card Insertion and Removal**: This section explains how to put your Moto G Power's SIM (Subscriber Identity Module) and SD (Secure Digital) cards in and out. While an SD card enables you to increase your capacity for movies and apps, a SIM card is required for access to cellular networks.

• **Add or Remove Accounts**: This section explains how to add various account kinds, including Google or email accounts, to your phone and how to delete them when necessary. This makes it possible for contacts, emails, calendar events, and other data to be synchronized between devices.

• **Set Up Voicemail**: You may configure your voicemail service in this part. In order to receive messages when you're not accessible, you must first set up a password and greeting.

• **Set Up Email**: This is where you configure your device's email accounts (Outlook, Gmail, etc.). The phone will sync your contacts, inbox, and outbox for convenient access when you follow instructions to input your credentials.

Personalize it to your Taste.

• Customize Your Home Screen: This section describes how to alter the layout of your home screen to your liking, add or remove apps, and rearrange icons.

• **Wallpaper Change**: Find out how to alter the background on your lock screen or home screen. You may accomplish this by either choosing a picture from your phone's gallery or by utilizing the default wallpaper that comes with your device.

• **Add Folders, Shortcuts, or Widgets**: Widgets let you add interactive components to your home screen for easy access, such as the calendar or weather. You may access apps or features directly via shortcuts. By keeping programs in one location, folders help you clear up screen clutter.

• **Modify additional Home Settings**: For a more customized interface, you may modify additional home screen settings in this area, including the grid size, icon shape, and display settings.

• **Lock Screen**: You may customize how your phone acts while it is locked by going into the lock screen settings. Both the information shown and the way your phone responds to touch may be changed.

• **Use a Screen Saver**: Find out how to set up a screen saver that shows the time, pictures, or other data when your phone is charging or not in use.

• **Sounds**: All audio-related options, including ringtones, alarms, and notification sounds, are covered in this area.

o Modify Notification Sounds and Ringtone: You may set distinct sounds for alerts (such as emails or messages) and alter the ringtone for calls on your smartphone.

o **Modify Volume Settings**: Change the volume of the system, media, and ringer noises on your phone.

o Configure "Do Not Disturb," a function that turns off calls and notifications when you're sleeping or in meetings, for example.

• Display: Your device's visual settings are covered in this section.

o **Adjust Screen Brightness**: Modify the screen's brightness to suit your surroundings. You have the option to manually change the brightness or select auto-brightness for automatic adjustments.

o **Modify Font and Display Size**: To make text and other UI components simpler to read or navigate, adjust their sizes.

o **Modify Theme**: To lessen eye strain or to suit your tastes, you can switch the theme from light to dark mode.

o **Modify Screen Timeout**: Modify the amount of time your phone remains on after being inactive before shutting off on its own.

o **Select Color Mode**: To improve the visual experience, you may alter your screen's color settings, such as choosing a warm or cold tone.

o **Modify Screen Colors at Night**: By modifying the screen's color temperature at night, you may lessen your exposure to blue light and lessen eye strain.

• **Gestures**: These touch-based movements let you navigate your phone more easily.

o **operate One-Handed Mode**: This feature makes it easier to operate the screen with only one hand by allowing you to resize and shift its contents to one side.

o **Take a snapshot**: Learn how to capture a snapshot of your screen, which may be used to store material or share it with others.

o **Use Quick Settings**: From the top of your screen, Quick Settings offers shortcuts to key features like Bluetooth, Wi-Fi, and Do Not Disturb.

o **Making use of Split-Screen Multitasking**: Split-screen makes multitasking simpler by enabling you to utilize two programs at once.

• **Use Screen Lock**: By requiring a PIN, password, pattern, or biometric identification (such as a fingerprint) to access your phone, screen lock helps keep your phone safe.

o **Configure Fingerprint Recognition**: Without entering a PIN, you may swiftly and safely unlock the device by registering your fingerprint.

o **Configure Face Unlock**: This function offers a quick and safe method of accessing your smartphone by using face recognition to unlock it.

o **Lock SIM Card**: Adding a PIN to your SIM card increases security in the event that your phone is stolen or misplaced. The SIM card cannot be used in other devices without the PIN.

o **Use Find My Device**: If your phone is stolen or misplaced, you may find it using this tool. To preserve your privacy, you may remotely lock it, track its position, or delete its data.

You can safeguard your data, use advanced functions effectively, and customize your Moto G Power by following this tutorial, which covers both the basic setup and customization choices.

Discover the Fundamentals

• About Your Home Screen: In this part, you will learn about the Moto G Power's home screen layout, which includes widgets, applications, and shortcuts. It offers a summary of how to use and navigate the tools and applications on the screen.

· **About Your Lock Screen**: Discover how your device's lock screen works, including how to personalize it and how it responds when it is locked. Additionally, you will discover whether you have security measures like a PIN or pattern lock set up, as well as easy access options like camera shortcuts and alerts.

• **Are you new to Android**? This section offers a basic overview of Android for those who are unfamiliar with Android smartphones. Gestures, navigation, and key features like the app drawer, notification bar, and multitasking will all be covered.

• **Use Accessibility Features**: Users with impairments may learn how to activate different accessibility features in this area. Visual aids, hearing aids, and other tools that facilitate the device's use are examples of these characteristics.

o **Visual Assistance**: Tools to help people with visual impairments, such as screen readers, high contrast text, and gestures for magnification.

o **Hearing Assistance**: Provides features that assist users with hearing problems, such as visual feedback for sound and compatibility with hearing aids.

o **Dexterity Assistance**: Features like activating physical switches or moving to a bigger touch target are intended to assist users who struggle with touchscreens.

• **Make Use of Accessibility Shortcuts**: These are easy methods to use a single tap or gesture to turn on or off certain accessibility features. For simpler access to the functions you use most, this section describes how to configure and utilize these shortcuts.

Advanced Functionalities

• Camera: A thorough how-to manual for the Moto G Power's camera. The several camera modes and settings will be covered in this part, along with advice on how to take excellent pictures and films.

o **snap a Picture**: Acquire the skills necessary to snap pictures in many modes, such as panorama, night, and portrait. Autofocus and other camera settings that might improve your images will also be covered.

o **Edit Photos and Videos**: You can use the phone's built-in features to edit photos or videos after you've taken them. This covers video cutting, cropping, filtering, and brightness adjustments.

• **Google Account**: How to add and manage your Google account on your phone is covered in this section. Contacts, emails, calendars, and other Google services like Gmail, Drive, and the Play Store may all be synced with a Google account.

• **Google Lens**: This tool recognizes items and provides more details about them by using the camera. By aiming your camera at comparable objects, you may use this tool to translate languages, read text, search for products, and more.

• **Google One**: This online storage solution gives you additional room for your documents, movies, and images. The setup and management of your storage plans are covered in this section.

• **Google Assistant**: Discover how to utilize this AI-powered voice assistant, which can be used to create reminders, send texts, obtain directions, and answer queries using voice commands.

• **Create a Contact Widget**: To provide easy access to crucial contacts, you may make a shortcut on your home screen. The creation and usage of contact widgets are described in this section.

• **Nearby exchange**: This function uses Bluetooth or Wi-Fi to let you to exchange files, images, and links with devices that are close by. To make sharing with friends and coworkers simple, you will learn how to set it up and utilize it.

• **Office Features**: The office tools on your phone, including Google Docs, Sheets, Slides, and other productivity apps, are covered in this section. These tools let you create and edit documents while you're on the move.

• **Printing**: With a suitable printer, you can print documents, images, and other files straight from your Moto G Power. How to connect your phone to a printer and begin printing is covered in this section.

• **Split-Screen Multitasking**: By splitting the screen into two parts, this function enables you to utilize two apps simultaneously. It works really well for multitasking, like viewing a movie while using the internet.

• **Configure and Manage a VPN**: Discover how to configure a Virtual Private Network (VPN) on your device so that you may browse the internet safely. Particularly while utilizing public Wi-Fi, a VPN protects your privacy and security by encrypting your internet connection.

• **Screenshots**: To record what's on your screen, follow these steps to learn how to take screenshots on your smartphone. After that, you may store the snapshot for later use or share it.

• **Security**: Find out how your device's security features help safeguard your privacy and data. This covers how to manage app permissions, use biometrics (facial recognition and fingerprints), and lock your screen.

o **Screen Lock**: Using a PIN, pattern, password, or biometric lock, you may safeguard your phone using this setting. It keeps your device safe from unwanted access.

o **Fingerprint Recognition**: Enable fingerprint recognition on your phone to unlock it and carry out safe operations like approving payments or opening apps.

o facial Unlock: To provide an extra degree of ease and security, unlock your phone using facial recognition.

o **Google Play Protect**: By routinely checking your phone's apps for any dangers, this function helps shield your device against harmful apps.

• **Location**: This section describes how to control the location services on your device.

o **Use Location Services**: Discover how to make your device's location services active or inactive. This makes it possible for apps that use your current position, like maps or ride-sharing services, to deliver more precise information.

o **Configure Emergency Information**: You may add crucial emergency details to your phone, such allergies, medical issues, or emergency contacts. In an emergency, you may obtain this information via your lock screen.

Both the basic functions of your Moto G Power and more sophisticated options to enhance and customize your experience are covered in these areas.

Chapter 2: Telephone Calls

• **Make a Call**: The Moto G Power makes making calls simple. You may choose a contact from your contacts list or use the Phone app to dial a number directly. Additionally, the Phone app offers a search function that makes it easy to locate contacts.

o **Dialing a Number:** Launch the Phone app, hit the call button after entering the number and tapping the dial pad.

o To call a contact, press the Contacts tab, pick the person you wish to reach, and then tap their number.

• **Answer and End Calls**: The name or number of the caller appears on the screen when you answer an incoming call. You have two options:

o To accept the call, press or swipe the green answer button.

o To reject or terminate the call, use the red hang-up button.

• **Call Waiting**: You will be alerted by a sound or vibration if a new call comes in while you are on an active call. You can then decide whether to accept the new call and place the first on hold or to deny it.

• **Speakerphone**: You may share the discussion with others or converse hands-free by touching the speaker icon to activate the speakerphone feature during a call.

• **Call forwarding**: In the event that you are unavailable, calls can be sent from your phone to another number. You may configure this under Call Forwarding in your call settings.

• **Voicemail**: When you miss a call, voicemail lets you get messages. Voicemail allows callers to leave a message if you are not available. You may use your carrier's voicemail app or call your voicemail to listen to and manage voicemail messages.

• **Call Blocking**: You may use the Call Blocking option in your settings to stop unsolicited calls from a certain number or contact. For further spam prevention, you may either manually block numbers or utilize a third-party program.

• **Conference Calls**: To hold a conference call, you can join several calls at once. This is usually accomplished by taking the second call after placing the previous one on hold. You may combine the calls into a single discussion on the majority of smartphones.

Chapter 3: Text messages, including MMS and SMS

• **Send a Text Message**: You may send MMS (Multimedia Messaging Service) or SMS (Short Message Service) messages using the Messages app.

To convey a message:

1. Launch the app called Messages.

2. To begin a new chat, use the + (compose) button.

3. Either choose a contact or enter the recipient's phone number.

4. Press Send after entering your message in the text box.

• **Send Multimedia Messages**: MMS may be used to send an audio clip, video, or picture. Just pick the file you wish to share, touch the attachment symbol (a paperclip or camera icon), and then tap share.

• **Group Messaging:** By adding many contacts to the recipient list, you may send group SMS. Group conversations benefit from this functionality, however be aware that MMS fees may apply according on your carrier.

• **Responding to Messages**: To read a text message, use the Messages app and touch on the message thread. After that, you may type and submit a response. Additionally, you may respond straight from the notice.

• **Quick Replies**: Without launching the Messages app, you may reply to messages on the Moto G Power right from the notification. When you're busy, this is excellent for responding quickly.

• **Message Notifications**: Depending on your preferences, your phone may vibrate, play noises, or display pop-up alerts when new messages arrive. The Settings app's Notifications section allows you to personalize the way that messages are delivered.

• **Archived Conversations**: You can archive a message thread if you no longer want to view it in your inbox but don't want to remove it. Archiving preserves the data while moving the discussion to a secret folder. The Messages app allows you to view conversations that have been archived.

• **Ban or Report Spam**: Within the texts app, you have the option to ban a number or report it as spam if you're getting unsolicited or spam texts. This function aids in removing spam communications in the future.

• **Message Search**: The Messages app offers an integrated search feature that lets you go through your conversation history by contact name or keywords if you're looking for a specific message.

• **Text Message Settings**: You can change the way your messages are sent and received in the Messages app. You can change the font size of your messages, enable or disable SMS delivery reports, or activate advanced features like Rich Communication Services (RCS), which offers improved features like read receipts and typing indicators (available with supported carriers).

• **Plan a Message**: Text messages can be planned to be sent at a later time. When you're not available, this tool is helpful for delivering messages or reminders.

• **Emoji, Stickers, and GIFs**: Use emojis, stickers, or GIFs to inject your texts with humorous or emotive content. You can choose from these in the text input field.

Extra Features for Texting and Calling

• Dual SIM (if supported): You can control two separate phone numbers on a single Moto G Power if it has dual SIM capability. You may control the contacts linked to each SIM card and decide which SIM card to use for outgoing calls and texts.

You may have incoming text messages read aloud to you by using the Text-to-Speech

(TTS) capability. This is helpful if you can't glance at your phone screen while driving. The accessibility options on the phone allow you to enable it.

• **Emergency notifications**: Weather, safety, and other significant events will trigger emergency notifications on your phone. You will be alerted by sound or vibration when these messages show up on your screen.

• **Visual Voicemail**: This feature, which lets you view a list of voicemail messages with information like caller ID and message length, is supported by some carriers. After that, you may decide which messages to save, delete, or listen to.

You may maximize the Moto G Power's call and text messaging capabilities by being aware of and setting up these options.

Chapter 4: The camera

Your Moto G Power's camera is loaded with capabilities that will help you take excellent pictures and movies. To make the most of it, follow these steps:

Snap a Photo
• Open the Camera App: Either slide up from the home screen to access your applications, then tap the Camera app, or hit the Camera icon on your home screen to open the camera.

• **Take a Picture**: After the camera is open, frame your image and press the shutter button, which is represented by a circle. By swiping left or right on the screen, you may navigate between several camera settings, such as Photo, Portrait, Night, and Panorama.

• **Use the Front-Facing Camera**: Tap the camera flip symbol, which is often a circular arrow, in the camera interface to switch between the front and back cameras. For video chats and selfies, the front camera is perfect.

Modify Pictures and Videos

• Basic Editing: To make changes to a photo after it has been taken, hit the edit icon, which is typically a pencil or magic wand icon. This enables you to apply filters, crop, rotate, and change the brightness.

• **Advanced Editing**: You may also add unique effects like sepia or black-and-white tones, as well as change contrast, saturation, and sharpness. If you want to improve the quality of your photos or videos before sharing them, this is helpful.

Modes of the Camera

The usual camera mode for shooting images is called "Photo Mode." To take sharp, colorful pictures, it automatically modifies parameters like exposure and white balance.

• **Portrait Mode**: This setting gives your images a polished depth-of-field look by focusing on the topic in the foreground and blurring the background. Selfies and pictures of individuals are frequently taken in this mode.

• **Night Mode**: This feature improves low-light photography by combining many exposures to produce a sharper, brighter image in low light. Night mode guarantees that your pictures will still seem sharp even if you're in a dark setting.

• **Panorama Mode**: This enables you to capture large, expansive landscape images. The phone's camera will stitch the shots together to produce a panoramic picture if you move it from side to side.

• **Pro Mode**: For more complex photography, Pro Mode allows you to manually alter parameters like ISO, exposure, and focus if you want complete control.

• **Video Recording**: To begin recording videos, tap the video symbol, which is a red circle. While filming, you may switch between the front and back cameras and change the resolution. Additionally, you may zoom in and out when recording a video.

• **Slow Motion**: Choose the Slow Motion setting to record slow-motion footage. For dramatic effect, you may use this to record fast-moving objects or movements and play them back at a slower pace.

• **Time Lapse**: This technique allows you to shoot a number of pictures at predetermined intervals and combine them to create a little film that illustrates the passage of time.

• **Macro option**: This option enables you to clearly catch minute objects and complex textures by having the camera focus on little details from a very close distance.

Extra Features of the Camera

• **Google Lens**: You may use Google Lens to recognize images when in Camera mode. Google Lens will display pertinent data or search results when you aim your camera at objects, text, or landmarks.

• **HDR (High Dynamic Range)**: HDR balances the exposure of both bright and dark regions in your images. It assists photographs that could otherwise have underexposed shadows or overexposed highlights by adding additional detail.

• **Face and Smile Detection**: To make sure your subjects are in focus, the camera employs face detection. When the camera senses a grin, it may immediately start taking pictures.

• **Filters and Effects**: Before snapping a picture, you may use real-time filters to change color saturation, contrast, and creative effects like black and white or sepia.

Gallery

You can see, arrange, and control all of the pictures and videos you've made with your Moto G Power camera using the Gallery app. Here's how to get around it:

See Pictures and Videos

• **Launch the Gallery App**: To launch the Gallery app, tap its icon from your app drawer or home screen.

• **Album Organization**: Using a variety of categories, including screenshots, camera photographs, WhatsApp images, and more, the Gallery app groups your photos into albums. To arrange your material whatever you choose, you may even make your own albums.

• **Timeline View**: Typically, images are shown chronologically, with the most recent images at the top. You may browse your photos and videos by scrolling through your timeline.

• **Sort by Date or kind**: To locate certain material fast, you may sort your media in the Gallery settings by date, album, or kind (pictures, videos, or screenshots).

Modify Images in the Gallery

• Crop and Rotate: Tap a photo to bring up the full-screen view for editing. You may crop, rotate, or reorient the image by tapping the edit icon.

• **Use Filters:** You may use filters in the Gallery to improve the appearance of your images, just as in the Camera app. Select from options such as creative styles, sepia, or black-and-white.

• **Modify Brightness, Contrast, and More**: Make adjustments to the image's exposure, contrast, and saturation using the adjustment tools.

• **Add Text and Stickers:** Before sharing, you may add amusing words or stickers to your images to make them more unique.

Exchange Pictures and Videos

• **Share via Email or Messaging**: You may send photos or videos straight from the Gallery to your email, messaging applications, or social networking accounts

(Facebook, Instagram, etc.). Select the app or method of your choice by tapping on the share icon.

• **Make Albums**: To arrange your material, you may make new albums. Select the images or videos you wish to add by tapping the Add symbol in the Gallery's Albums section.

Remove and Organize Pictures

• **Delete**: Tap and hold a photograph, then choose the trash symbol to remove undesirable photos. Additionally, you may choose numerous photographs in batch mode to erase them all at once.

• **Archive**: You can archive a photo to make it invisible without erasing it. Archived images won't be removed from your phone; instead, they will be transferred to a different area of the app.

• **Retrieve Deleted Files**: You may retrieve deleted files from the Gallery's Trash folder if you unintentionally erased anything. Before being permanently deleted, deleted media will be kept here for 30 days.

Make a Slideshow

• **Make and Play a Slideshow**: You may make a slideshow by choosing several images or videos. Select the parameters that you want, such the music to go with the slideshow or the transition effects.

Look for Images and Videos

• **Search Function**: To discover certain photographs fast, the Gallery app has a search function that lets you look for photos based on dates, places, or even phrases like "beach" or "birthday."

Integration with Google Photos

• **Cloud Backup**: All of your pictures and videos may be automatically backed up to the cloud if you have Google Photos installed. This guarantees that, even in the event that you misplace or break your device, your material will be securely preserved.

Your Moto G Power's Camera and Gallery applications give you strong tools for capturing, processing, arranging, and sharing images and movies. With the aid of these tools, you may easily record every moment and retrieve your material at any time.

Phone Configuration

You may modify a number of system settings and customize the operation of your Moto G Power using the Settings app. You may adjust every feature of your phone with the Settings app, including network connections, display settings, security settings, and more.

Internet & Network

• Wi-Fi: Turn on Wi-Fi and choose a network to connect to wireless networks. Additionally, you may modify advanced Wi-Fi settings, manage stored Wi-Fi networks, and create a Wi-Fi hotspot to share your mobile data with others.

• **Mobile Network**: Use this link to control your mobile data connection. You may configure tools like Data Saver to restrict data use, select your network provider, and activate or disable mobile data.

• **Bluetooth**: To connect to wireless devices such as speakers, headphones, or other gadgets that support Bluetooth, turn Bluetooth on or off.

• **Airplane Mode**: To turn off all wireless connections simultaneously (including Bluetooth, Wi-Fi, and mobile data), switch on Airplane mode. This is particularly helpful in places with spotty coverage or on airplanes.

• **Virtual Private Network (VPN):** This section allows you to configure and control a VPN if you use one for safe internet access.

Devices Connected

• **USB Settings**: Choose the charging or file transfer modes to control how your device operates while connected to a computer via USB.

• **Casting**: Use Chromecast or another casting service to project your screen onto a TV or other device. This enables you to stream media or mirror the screen of your phone.

Bluetooth devices, including wireless keyboards, headphones, and other peripherals, may be paired and controlled.

Chapter 5: Applications

• **App Permissions**: Manage which apps on your phone can access specific features like the microphone, contacts, location, and camera.

• **App Notifications**: Adjust notification settings for specific applications, enabling you to silence or modify how each app informs you.

• **Default Apps**: To avoid having to choose an app each time, set default apps for tasks like messaging, web browsing, and video playback.

Show

• **Brightness**: Manually adjust the screen's brightness or turn on Adaptive Brightness to have it change automatically according to your surroundings.

• **Dark Mode**: Use a darker color scheme for menus and applications to lessen eye strain.

• **Screen Timeout**: Configure how long the screen remains active following your most recent interaction with it. The time range you can select from a few seconds to a few minutes.

• **Font Size & Display Size**: To make text and interface components easier to read, adjust the font and display sizes.

• **Screen Saver**: When your phone is idle or charging, turn on a screen saver to show pictures, artwork, or other visual components.

Vibration and Sound

• Ringtone: Select from a variety of preset sounds or original songs to customize your ringtone, notification sound, or alarm tone.

• **Vibration**: You can configure the phone to vibrate for calls and notifications rather than utilizing sound, or you may change the vibration strength for different alerts.

• **Do Not Disturb**: Configure "Do Not Disturb" mode to turn off all calls, alerts, and notifications during particular periods or occasions (such as meetings or sleep).

Location & Security

• **Screen Lock**: To stop unwanted access, set up a security lock on your phone using a pattern, PIN, or password.

• **Fingerprint Recognition & Face Unlock**: Set up biometric security options, like fingerprint or face recognition, for a quick and secure way to unlock your phone.

• **Find My Device**: Enable Find My Device to help you find your phone in case it's misplaced or stolen. You can follow your phone's position on a map, lock it remotely, or wipe your data to preserve your privacy.

• **Location**: Control location services for applications, such navigation apps or location-based services, that require your geographic location.

Accounts

• **Google Account**: Add and manage your Google account for access to Gmail, Google Drive, Google Photos, and other Google services. You can sync your contacts, calendar, and other information with your account.

• **Additional Accounts**: Include and oversee additional email accounts, such as Yahoo, Microsoft Exchange, or third-party email providers.

System

• **Software Updates**: To make sure your phone is running the most recent software version, check for system updates. This will cover security updates, new features, and performance enhancements.

• **Reset Options**: You can perform specific resets (like resetting network settings or app preferences) or return your phone to its factory settings if it's giving you trouble.

• About Phone: See key information about your phone, such as the model number, IMEI number, Android version, and more.

Quick Settings

Without navigating to the full Settings app, you can quickly access necessary controls and toggle important features using the Quick Settings menu. From the top of the screen, swipe down to access Quick Settings.

Quick Settings Toggles

• **Wi-Fi**: Toggle your Wi-Fi connection on or off with a single press. Additionally, by tapping the Wi-Fi icon, you can easily access available Wi-Fi networks.

• **Bluetooth**: Turn Bluetooth on or off with one swipe to connect or detach wireless devices like headphones and speakers.

• **Do Not Disturb**: Activate or disable Do Not Disturb mode, which silences calls and alerts. By touching and holding the symbol, you may also change how Do Not Disturb operates.

• **Airplane Mode**: To turn off all wireless functions, including Bluetooth, Wi-Fi, and mobile data, quickly switch Airplane Mode on or off.

• **Flashlight**: To activate or deactivate your phone's LED flashlight, tap this symbol. When you need a flashlight, here is an easy method to utilize your phone.

• **Rotation of the Screen**: Select between manual and automated rotation. This feature controls whether the screen rotates when you turn your phone sideways.

• **Battery Saver**: When your battery is low, turn on Battery Saver mode to minimize power usage and limit background programs. Your current battery % is also shown.

• **Location**: Easily activate or deactivate your location services. When location-based apps are not required, this can help save battery life.

• **Mobile Data**: Toggle mobile data on or off. This is especially important when you're controlling your data consumption or attempting to preserve battery.

• **Night Light**: Enable Night Light to reduce blue light and make your phone's display warmer, which can reduce eye strain, especially before bed.

• **Rotation Lock**: Prevent your screen from turning when you turn your phone by switching the Auto-rotate option on or off.

• **VPN**: If you use a VPN, you can easily login or detach by toggling the VPN symbol.

• **Volum**e: Adjust the phone's volume with a fast swipe to regulate media, call, and notification noises. You can set the volume for each individually.

• **Cast**: Tap the Cast icon to immediately start screen casting if you wish to share your phone's screen with a TV or other suitable device.

Accessing More Quick Settings

You may adjust the Quick Settings menu by tapping the Edit icon or by swiping down farther to get other choices. The icons may be added, removed, or rearranged to fit your needs.

You can quickly and easily adjust important functions with Quick Settings, and you can go further into your device's settings using the Settings app to make sure your Moto G Power operates the way you want it to.

Security and Biometrics on Moto G Power

To protect your device, data, and private information, security and biometrics are crucial. In addition to biometric capabilities like fingerprint recognition and face unlock, the Moto G Power has many choices for securing your phone using more conventional techniques like passwords and PINs.

Chapter 6: Configuration for Security

The Settings app's Security section gives you control over how your Moto G Power is shielded from unwanted access. Below is a summary of the primary choices:

Options for Screen Lock

1.PIN: To unlock your smartphone, you input a PIN, which is a numerical number that usually consists of four to six digits. Many people find it to be safe and speedy. To create a PIN:

o Select Screen lock under Settings > Security.

o To create the PIN you want, choose PIN and adhere to the instructions.

2.Password: An alphanumeric password, which consists of a mix of letters, numbers, and symbols, is an option if you want a more intricate security system. Compared to a PIN, this approach offers more security.

o Select Screen lock under Settings > Security.

To establish a safe password, select a password and follow the instructions.

3.**Pattern**: A pattern lock is a grid of interconnected dots that you may set. Although this is an entertaining and visually appealing method of protecting your smartphone, if someone watches you unlocking your phone, it can be simpler to figure out than a PIN or password.

o Select Screen lock under Settings > Security.

o Select a pattern and make your own unique unlock pattern.

4.When you're at home or using a linked item (such a Bluetooth watch or headphone), for example, you may use Smart Lock to keep your device unlocked in certain trusted scenarios. The ease of not having to unlock your phone each time is provided by this.

o Select Smart Lock under Settings > Security.

o Configure on-body detection, trusted locations, or trusted devices (which keeps your phone unlocked whether it's in your hand or pocket).

Notifications on the Lock Screen

• Lock Screen Preferences: You have the option to display sensitive alerts on the lock screen or not. For instance, you may configure it to display a quick overview of alerts or conceal the contents of incoming messages until the device is unlocked.

o To modify the way notifications show up on your lock screen, navigate to Settings > Security > Notifications.

Biometrics (Face Unlock and Fingerprint)

Face unlock and fingerprint recognition are two biometric identification techniques that your Moto G Power supports. These offer a quicker and safer method of unlocking your phone.

Recognition of Fingerprints

You may quickly and securely unlock your smartphone using fingerprint recognition instead of remembering a pattern, password, or PIN.

1.Configure the Fingerprint Recognition System:

o Go to Settings > Security > Fingerprint.

o To register your fingerprint, adhere to the on-screen directions. To guarantee a correct scan, you will be required to place your finger on the fingerprint sensor many times.

2.**Fingerprinting for Other Purposes**:

o After registering, you may use your fingerprint to sign in to applications, authorize purchases from the Google Play Store, and unlock your phone, among other things.

o You can control which applications or features will use your fingerprint for authentication in the Fingerprint settings.

3.**Sensitivity to fingerprints**:

o You can try again or use a different finger if your fingerprint isn't recognized the first time. For convenient access with various fingers, you can add more than one fingerprint.

To get the best recognition, make sure your fingertips are dry and clean. Dirt or moisture may be the cause of the sensor's poor fingerprint reading.

Unlocking the Face

Face unlock enables you to quickly unlock your phone using facial recognition technology.

1.Configure Face Unlock:

o Select Face Unlock under Settings > Security.

o In the event that facial recognition doesn't work, you'll be prompted to set up a screen lock (PIN, password, or pattern).

o To enable the camera to scan your facial features, you must place your face in front of it during the setup process. Your face will be recognized by the phone and stored for later unlocking.

2.**How to Use Face Unlock**:

o You can unlock your phone by just gazing at the screen after face unlock is configured. Your face is scanned by the front camera, and it will unlock automatically if it matches the registered face.

o Face unlock is fast, but it's crucial to remember that it might not function in some lighting situations or if you have your face obscured by something (like glasses or a mask).

3.**Improve Recognition**:

o In Face Unlock settings, you can retake your facial scan to improve the accuracy of the recognition process if it's not unlocking as quickly or accurately as you expect.

4.**Security Points to Remember**:

o Although face unlock is practical, it might not be as safe as fingerprint recognition because anyone can unlock your phone by holding it up to your face, particularly in well-lit areas.

o If security is an issue for you, think about making fingerprint recognition your main unlocking method or turning on a screen lock as a fallback in case face recognition doesn't work.

Other Security Features
Lock SIM Card

The SIM card lock adds an extra degree of protection by requesting a PIN to unlock your SIM card when restarting or putting it into a new phone.

1.**Enable SIM Lock**:

o Go to Settings > Security > SIM card lock.

o Enter the PIN for your SIM card to set it up. Once enabled, you'll need to enter the PIN each time the phone is powered on.

Find My Device

To preserve your privacy, you may remotely trace the position of your Moto G Power, lock it, or even remove your data if you misplace it. You may use another device to find your phone with Google's Find My Device feature.

1.**Turn on "Find My Device"**:

o Select Find My Device under Settings > Security.

o Make sure the functionality is enabled so you may use a Google Account to track the position of your phone.

2.Monitoring and Actions at a Distance:

o To utilize Find My smartphone, visit the Find My Device website or use the Find My Device app from another Android smartphone. Here, you may monitor the phone's position on a map, call the phone, lock it remotely, or wipe your data to prevent illegal access.

Google Play Protect

Google Play Protect is an in-built security feature that helps protect your phone from harmful apps, malware, and other security threats by scanning apps for potential risks.

1.Enable Google Play Protect:

o Go to Settings > Security > Google Play Protect.

o Verify that Play Protect is on so that apps are automatically scanned for vulnerabilities or dangerous behavior.

Best Practices for Security

1.Use Two-Factor Authentication (2FA): For services like your Google account, use two-factor authentication to offer an extra degree of protection.

2.**Update Software Regularly**: Keep your Moto G Power up-to-date by applying the latest security patches and software updates. This will help safeguard your device from vulnerabilities.

3.**Use Secure Apps**: Download apps only from reliable sources like the Google Play Store and be aware of apps that require excessive rights.

By using the security and biometric capabilities on your Moto G Power, you can keep your smartphone and personal data safe from illegal access, while enjoying easy and quick unlocking methods like fingerprint recognition and face unlock.

Notification Panel on Moto G Power

Your Moto G Power's Notification Panel is a crucial feature that offers shortcuts to vital settings and instant access to notifications, messages, and alarms. You may use it to keep informed and take action without having to open any particular menus or apps.

Getting to the Notification Panel

Swipe down from the top of the screen to see the Notification Panel. To see more options, slide down twice to completely expand the panel, or swipe down once for a fast look.

Alerts

You can stay informed about what's going on on your phone via notifications, which are alerts or updates from apps and system services. They may originate from calendar events, emails, social media, messaging applications, system updates, or even weather warnings.

• **How Notifications Look**: When you get notifications, they show up at the top of the screen as cards or banners.

o Text Notifications: You will get a synopsis of the content of emails or texts.

o **App Alerts**: Short messages and symbols are displayed in notifications from applications such as Facebook, Instagram, and WhatsApp.

o **Ongoing alerts**: As long as an application or music player is running, some alerts will be displayed in the notification area.

Making Use of Notifications:

o Swipe Away: Swipe a notification left or right to dismiss it.

o Respond or Take Action: Without launching the app, you may reply to certain alerts, such an email or text message. You can take action by tapping on the notice to accomplish this.

o **Expand Notifications**: To display more information, some notifications, particularly emails or messages, can be expanded. You can expand the notification for more information or tap on it to open it completely.

Handle Notification Management:

o To view a notification's settings, long-press on it. Notifications from some applications can be muted, turned off, or their banner design, sound, or vibration changed.

o App Notifications Settings: Select Settings > Apps & Notifications > Notifications to control how particular apps send alerts. Any app's notifications may be turned off or altered here.

Panel for Quick Settings

You can toggle common settings on and off with a single tap using the shortcuts found in the Quick Settings panel, which is a part of the Notification Panel. This is a practical method of changing settings without launching the Settings app in its entirety.

Icons for Quick Settings

Icons appear at the top of the Notification Panel when you swipe down. These stand for various features that you may easily enable or disable. Below is a summary of the most often used icons:

1.**Wi-Fi**: Turn it on and off. To swiftly connect to available networks, tap the Wi-Fi icon.

2.**Bluetooth**: Turn Bluetooth on or off. Tap to connect or detach from Bluetooth devices like headphones, speakers, or other accessories.

3.Do Not Disturb: Silence calls, notifications, and alerts. You can tap and hold to customize how Do Not Disturb works (e.g., allowing calls from certain contacts).

4.Turn off all wireless connections, such as Bluetooth, Wi-Fi, and mobile data, while in airplane mode. When traveling or in places with poor connectivity, it's helpful.

5.**Flashlight**: Turn on the LED flash on the back of your phone to use as a flashlight.

6.**Location**: Turn on or off location services. To change how applications can access your location, tap.

7.**Battery Saver**: To reduce background operations and prolong battery life, activate Battery Saver mode.

8.**Screen Rotation Lock**: To stop your phone from turning as you move it, lock the screen orientation.

9.Night Light: Turn on Night Light to warm the screen and lessen blue light, which is better for the eyes at night.

10.Mobile Data: Activate or deactivate mobile data. When on Wi-Fi, tap to control data consumption or turn it off.

11.Cast: If you wish to share your phone's screen with a TV or another device, press here to immediately start casting.

12. **VPN**: Toggle your Virtual Private Network (VPN) connection on or off.

13. **Sound**: Adjust your phone's sound profile. Tap to mute, set to vibrate, or adjust volume levels for media, calls, and notifications.

14. **Volume**: Using the panel, control the phone's volume for calls, media, alerts, and alarms.

Increasing the Quick Settings Functionaties

You can see Quick Settings in full view with more options and more detailed adjustments if you slide down twice (or swipe down once and then hit the expand icon).

• **Customize Quick Settings**: You may add or delete certain toggles and alter the icon order. To accomplish this:

o To access the customizing mode, tap the pencil icon, also known as the Edit button.

o Drag the icons into new locations or take out any toggles that aren't needed.

o You can add icons for things like Screen Saver or Battery Saver, depending on your preferences.

Additional Features in the Notification Panel

1.**History of Notifications**:

o If you've dismissed alerts by accident, you may access them again by turning on Notification History.

Toggle this feature on by going to Settings > Apps & Notifications > Notifications > Notification History.

2.**Astute Reaction**:

o Some alerts let you respond right from the notice itself, such as those from messaging applications (like WhatsApp, SMS, etc.). Smart Reply makes prompt answer recommendations depending on the conversation's context.

3.Controls for the Media:

o The Notification Panel displays media controls (play/pause, skip, and volume) whether you are listening to music, podcasts, or videos. Without launching the media app, you may change the volume, pause, or skip tracks from the notification panel.

Taking Charge of Notifications in Greater Detail

Take the following actions to have more control over when and how you get notifications:

• Select Notifications under Settings > Apps & Notifications.

• Customize Notification Categories: Certain apps, like social media or messaging apps, provide various notification kinds (e.g., direct messages, mentions, or general updates). You may control these categories so that you only get the alerts that are most important to you.

• **Notification Style**: Depending on how you would like notifications to appear, select from a variety of notification styles, including pop-up and floating.

Summary

The Notification Panel on your Moto G Power is an easy-to-access, interactive environment where you can control alerts and settings. From app alerts and messages to fast settings like Wi-Fi, Bluetooth, and Do Not Disturb, the panel is designed to offer you with quick, simple access to critical features. By personalizing your alerts and quick settings, you can adapt the experience to your own requirements and effectively manage your smartphone while being informed.

Moto G Power Features and Applications

Numerous functions and programs (apps) are included with the Moto G Power to improve your user experience. These features and applications give you the resources you require for security, productivity, entertainment, and everyday chores. Below is a summary of the main applications and functions that your Moto G Power has to offer:

Moto G Power's pre-installed applications

These applications are ready to use right out of the box because they are pre-installed on your device. While some provide extra services or features, others are necessary for your phone to function.

Crucial Apps

1.Phone: The standard application for placing and receiving phone calls. You may access your voicemail, contacts, and call history with its assistance.

2.**Messages**: A messaging software that allows you to send and receive text messages (SMS) and multimedia messages (MMS). Additionally, group texts, images, and videos may be sent.

3.**Contacts**: Keeps track of all your contacts, including email addresses and phone numbers. It syncs contacts between devices by integrating with your Google account.

4.**Camera**: The built-in camera app for capturing images and videos. Additionally, it has sophisticated features like Night Vision, Panorama, and Portrait Mode.

5.View, arrange, and edit the images and videos you take with your Moto G Power in the gallery. You may distribute media through email or social networks as well.

6.**Calendar**: Make use of this tool to plan your appointments, events, and reminders. You may connect it with your Google account to access your calendar across many devices.

7.**Email**: The built-in email app allows you to send and receive emails from various accounts, including Gmail and non-Gmail accounts (like Yahoo or Outlook).

8.The Moto G Power's built-in web browser is Google Chrome. You can use it to save your favorite websites, browse the web, and conduct information searches.

9.You may download and install new applications, games, movies, books, and more from the Google Play Store.

10.File sharing and storage are made possible via Google Drive, a cloud storage service. It gives you access to your files across all of your devices and is connected with other Google services.

Custom Features and Moto Apps

Numerous Moto applications that improve the Android experience and let you personalize and optimize your phone are included with the Moto G Power.

1.**Moto Display**: Without unlocking the phone, Moto Display provides a practical method to view the time and notifications. On the lock screen, it displays incoming messages, alerts, and other data. Additionally, Moto Actions provides gesture-based phone interaction with features like Twist for Camera, Swipe to reduce screen, and Chop twice for flashlight.

2.**Moto Voice**: This software allows you operate your phone using voice commands. You can launch apps, send messages, make calls, and more simply by speaking to your phone, even when the screen is off.

3.**Moto Security:** With features like Find My smartphone, Screen Lock, and Fingerprint

Security, this software helps keep your smartphone safe. Additionally, it offers a Safe option that allows you to safely save important data.

4.**Moto File Manager**: An application that facilitates the management and arrangement of files on your phone, including music, videos, documents, and pictures. It allows you to move, delete, or copy files effortlessly and access them quickly.

5.**Moto Actions**: A series of customizable motions that make your phone more comfortable to operate. Among the actions are twist for instant camera access, chop twice for flashlight, and one-handed mode.

6.**Moto Music**: An integrated application for playing your music files. It enables you to play music straight from your phone, make playlists, and explore your music collection.

7.**Moto Notes**: An app for taking notes that lets you write and arrange links, text, and images.

Google Apps and Services

For a more connected and efficient experience, Moto G Power incorporates a number of Google Services. Your life will be easier with these features and apps that work throughout your Android ecosystem.

1.Your voice-activated AI helper is Google helper. It may be programmed to do a number of things, including as sending SMS, answering questions, managing smart devices, and setting reminders. Saying "Hey Google" or holding down the home button will activate it, which is incorporated throughout your phone.

2.**Google Maps**: An effective navigation tool that assists you in finding locations of interest, traffic data, and instructions. It may also be used to locate eateries, shops, and other places in the area.

3.**Google Photos**: A program that backs up your images and videos to the cloud automatically. It gives sophisticated capabilities to organize, edit, and search through your material.

4.**Google Calendar**: A reminder and event planning app. You may schedule and get reminders for meetings, events, and appointments, and it syncs with your Google account.

5.Google Keep is a note-taking application for making and managing brief notes, ideas, and checklists. It syncs between devices and may be viewed via the web or other Android smartphones.

6.**Google Drive**: Offers cloud storage for storing documents, files, and images. These files are accessible from any device that is linked to your Google account.

7.**Google Play Movies & TV**: A platform for purchasing or renting movies and TV shows. You may stream them on other devices or view them immediately on your Moto G Power.

8.Google Play Music is a music streaming service that lets you listen to podcasts and music or save your own songs.

Features of Entertainment and Productivity

Numerous apps that improve your entertainment and productivity are included with the Moto G Power.

Features for Entertainment

1.**YouTube**: Play music, videos, and other media. In order to share your own videos, like videos, and subscribe to channels, you may also register for a YouTube account.

2.**Spotify**: Use this well-known app to stream music and podcasts. You may make playlists and listen to millions of music or podcasts.

3.**Netflix**: A service that requires a membership to view movies, TV series, and original material. Get it straight from your mobile device.

4.**Amazon Prime Video**: With an Amazon Prime membership, you can view movies, TV series, and other exclusive content on this video streaming service.

Productivity Apps

1.Google Docs, Sheets, and Slides: Google's suite of office productivity tools for creating, editing, and sharing documents, spreadsheets, and presentations. They are completely integrated with Google Drive.

2.**Microsoft Office (Word, Excel, PowerPoint):** If you have a Microsoft 365 subscription or prefer working with Microsoft products, these applications allow you to access, create, and edit documents on the move.

3.The preferred program for viewing, annotating, and altering PDF documents is Adobe Acrobat Reader.

4.Google Keep is an easy-to-use note-taking app that allows you to take notes, create to-do lists, and set reminders.

Advanced Functionalities

For power users or those who want to get the most out of their device, the Moto G Power offers a number of additional functions in addition to the regular applications and functionality.

1.Using two programs side by side on the screen is known as split-screen multitasking. Open an app, then slide up and hold the app icon in the recent apps view to activate split-screen mode. Choose a different app to use on the opposite half of the screen after selecting Split Screen.

2.**Screen Recording**: To record gaming, software demos, or any other type of information, you may record your screen with the Moto G Power. Navigate to Quick Settings and select Screen Record to enable screen recording.

3.**VPN (Virtual Private Network):** Protect your privacy by utilizing a VPN service, which generates a private connection whether using public Wi-Fi or reading sensitive material. The Settings > Network & Internet > VPN menu allows you to configure and control a VPN.

Features of Security and Privacy

1.Face Unlock & Fingerprint Recognition: To secure your phone, set up biometric security features like fingerprint recognition or face unlock.

2.**Google Play Protect:** This integrated security tool checks your apps for vulnerabilities and malicious activity. In the Google Play Store settings, you can make it active.

3.**Find My Device**: A helpful tool that lets you find your misplaced phone, remotely lock it, or remove data to stop unwanted access.

4.**App Permissions**: In Settings > applications & Notifications > Permissions, you can manage which applications have access to private data, including your location, contacts, and camera.

In brief

Numerous functions and apps are included with your Moto G Power to make it a potent tool for productivity, entertainment, and security. The gadget is geared for daily use, with features like Moto Actions and Moto Display as well as Google services like Gmail and Google Drive. These apps and features may be extended, managed, and customized to meet your needs, guaranteeing a seamless and pleasurable experience.